BABYLON APOCALYPSE

STROKE

ENGLISH EDITION

> *There is nothing to writing. All you do is sit down at a typewriter and bleed.*
> Ernest Hemingway

> **For the land I live on. For the Neckar River. For the salmon, the otters, the stag beetles, the spotted salamanders. For the American bison, the European bison, the wolf, the bear, the lynx and all other victims of our culture. For the countless indigenous peoples who are victims of the ongoing genocide. For those people who are still able to feel sincere empathy and love. For Leo, my loving little sunshine, and for all the innocent little children who's future is being destroyed. For life on planet Earth. For Pacha Mama, Gaia, Mother Earth. My absolute loyalty belongs to you.**
> Stroke

Bibliografische Information der Deutschen Nationalbibliothek:
Die Deutsche Nationalbibliothek verzeichnet diese Publikation in der Deutschen Nationalbibliografie; detaillierte bibliografische Daten sind im Internet unter http://dnb.dnb.de abrufbar.

BABYLON APOCALYPSE
ISBN: 9783750420342

BabylonApocalypse.org

TABLE OF CONTENTS

THE MEGAMACHINE AS A FORM OF SOCIAL ORGANIZATION

On July 10th, 1985, the Rainbow Warrior, ship of the environmental organization Greenpeace, was sunk by agents of the French Service Action.

From the 1940's until the 60's, the US-Army had been testing atomic bombs on the Marshall Islands. What used to be a South Pacific paradise was now contaminated. The people suffered diseases and cancer, children were born with abnormalities. In 1985, the residents of the Island Rongelap asked Greenpeace for help. The Rainbow Warrior came and relocated 300 people to the Island of Mejato. From Mejato, the ship was supposed to move to New Zealand for a short stop and then to the Moruroa-atoll (French Polynesia) to protest against French atomic-bomb tests. While the Rainbow Warrior was anchored in the port of Aukland, New Zealand, during the night of July 10th, two bombs detonated in the ship's hull. While the ship sunk, most of the crew were able to save themselves, except for the photographer Fernando Pereira who drowned.[1] Tragically, he was parent of two small children.

The investigations of the New Zealand police lead to the French Secret Service. Under growing pressure, the government under Francois Mitterand steadily admitted being responsible for the attack.

In 1987, the French government paid a compensation of 8 million US-Dollars to Greenpeace and about 7 million to the New Zealand government. All of the people involved kept their positions in the French government, some received highest military honors.

In 1985, I was six years old. The pictures of the Rainbow Warrior were on the media everywhere. The Greenpeace activists were my heroes. I would look at the Greenpeace magazines that shocked me deeply with pictures of baby seals slain with clubs, burning rainforests and dead whales, swimming in a sea of blood.

If you take the perspective of a six or seven year old child, you see butts all around you and hear the voices of adults from above. In my memory, the adults spoke mostly about work.

"How was work?" "Well, ok..." "I have to work tomorrow." "Will you go to work?" "Yes." "I hear that you have a new job? How do you like it?"

---

1   "Pereira died, because the French Secret Service sunk a ship with people who where engaged in protecting the environment"
(Katja Iken in Spiegel: http://www.spiegel.de/einestages/rainbow-warrior-anschlag-auf-greenpeace-schiff-1985-a-1042273.html)

I felt there was a huge chasm between the conversations I overheard from the adults and the terrifying pictures that stuck in my childish mind from the Greenpeace magazines. They always wanted to know what I *want to become* when I grew up. The question is hard to understand for a seven year old. What should I become? I'm a human being already, and there is not much more I can actually become. Well, a grown-up human being, someday. But such a stressed out, worried adult, who is at the same time dependent on and plagued by his daily work, like the adults around me, I certainly didn't want to become. Why is their work so important to them, when at the same time such horrible things are happening?

Later, when I understood better what they were up to with that question, I always answered that I wanted to become an environmentalist, like the Greenpeace activists. After I learned to read and write, I printed myself business cards, stating *environmentalist* as profession.

Back then, questions evolved that didn't change much over all these years. Why do these people, by all costs, want to kill whales and seals? And why do they want to destroy these beautiful rainforests everywhere? And why are the people from Greenpeace obviously the only ones who care and try to stop the killing?[2]

I asked these questions as a child, but soon stopped, because I would never receive a satisfying answer. "You

---

2   Back in the days, Greenpeace still consisted mostly of real activists and was pretty radical. The organization has since been corrupted to be part of the non-governmental industrial complex and as such serves as vital part of industrial capitalism.

won't understand this, you are to small..." They would avoid my questions. They didn't like them. They were unpleasant for them, and they had no answers.

As a child, one tends to think that the grown-ups are very smart and know more than children. Unfortunately, this is a fraud. Most adults are very stupid, highly indoctrinated, and don't know any answers to the real important questions.

The questions remain the same, an I guess they will until the very day of my death. Why is our culture killing the planet? Why does nobody care about it? Why are people always talking about work, while there is a horrible slaughter going on?

When I asked my grandmother why all the Indians had to die, she answered that this had been God's will. The Indians, soon enough, would have built big ships on their own, sailed to Europe and exterminated us, she said. How great that God is with us!

Thanks to answers like this, I learned to forget my questions and hide my feelings over time, which, after all, arose from a very normal empathy I felt for our fellow beings, and indeed for the whole wonderful, unique planet we all inhabit .

I went through the mainstream culture with severe depressions. I held myself together with books, which helped me to survive disturbing dreams, think deeply and question everything. I will always be grateful to these writers.[3]

---

3   Erich Fromm, Derrick Jensen, Black Elk, John (Fire) Lame Deer, Vine Deloria Jr., Jack D. Forbes, Daniel Quinn, Henry David Thoreau...

Finally, I found myself realizing that the decision I had made when I was seven years old, to write *environmentalist* on my business card, was still right and valid.

Within a culture that mistreats its fellow creatures like ours, resistance is a moral imperative. I understood this as a child. Actually, it isn't very hard to understand. All we have to do is to look around us. Foolishly, we have built a whole culture based on distractions and denial.

It also has to do with the form of social organization this culture is based on, which might be the most destructive invention that humans have ever made. Gunpowder, for example, is surely a very destructive invention, especially if you use it, like our culture does, for weapons. Without firearms, it would have been far more difficult to drive big animals like bears, bison or Siberian tigers to the brink of extinction. Without firearms, the conquest of the Americas and the genocide of indigenous peoples worldwide would have been far more difficult. Firearms therefore take the second place on my rank of the most destructive inventions.

The plow and the combustion engine compete for the third place. While the wheel, which is often mentioned as one of the most important inventions, isn't very destructive by itself, the car, with all the surrounding "culture", infrastructure and industry, surely is one of the most destructive human artifacts. It is an extreme waste of energy to move a machine of about two tonnes of weight, most times only to transport one single human being. Car culture is the most energy intensive form of transportation that ever existed. We can only afford this unbelievable decadence because we learned to use fossil fuels for combustion engines. Apart from the waste of energy, it is also not very intelligent to poison the air that we need to breathe. It is a crime we commit to future generations.

> *"Technological inventions take from the earth but give nothing in return. Look at automobiles. They were, in a sense, dreamed up over a period of time, with different people adding on to each other's dreams — or, if you prefer, adding on to each other's studies and trials. But all along the way, very little, if anything, was given back to the hungry, invisible divinity that gave people the ability to invent those cars. Now, in a healthy culture, that's where the shamans would come in, because with every invention comes a spiritual debt that must be paid, either ritually, or else taken out of us in warfare, grief, or depression."*[4]
>
> *Martin Prechtel*

The plow stands for monocultural agriculture. I see agriculture as the blueprint of colonialism. They take a piece of land, drive away or kill all indigenous living beings, animals, humans and plants, and replace them with a monoculture of one species, individuals entirely brought into line.

In relation to that stands the most destructive invention humans ever made. Its not a technological innovation, but a form of social organization. Indeed a very technological form, and therefore called the megamachine.[5]

---

4   Saving The Indigenous Soul: An Interview With Martin Prechtel:
    http://www.derrickjensen.org/2001/04/saving-indigenous-soul-interview-martin-prechtel/
5   The term comes from Lewis Mumford's work "The myth of the machine", published in the 1960's

A form of social organization that makes is possible for a hundred thousand people to spend the majority of their lifetime happily working for the goals of giant corporations like Daimler-Benz, BASF, Bayer, Deutsche Bank et cetera. Hundreds of thousands of employees, working strictly organized and brought into line within a hierarchical organization. There often is a very strong identification of the employees with their company. This is the modern version of the social organization that made it possible for the ancient Egyptians to build the giant symbols of their civilization. In ancient Egypt, the slaves already formed an organized caste. They used strikes as a way to fight for better food, housing or working conditions. Even back then, people had already accepted their fate as a working class, as part of the machine, and tried to ensure slightly better conditions within it.

Slavery and agriculture are the cradle of civilization. Large-scale monoculture is only possible with slaves. Initially, slaves must be hold in captivity and forced to work. Nobody volunteers to be a slave, at least at the beginning. Over a few thousand years, our culture perfected the machine more and more. With a permanent combination of organized violence, lies, propaganda and powerful institutions like state, church and school, the original forms of social organization were destroyed and replaced with a breed of totally isolated human beings, who identify themselves as workers and do not resist any more. These are the happy slaves that serve the machine. Without them, factories are unthinkable, there would be no industrial agriculture, no machines, no industrial production. Nothing of this would be possible without the innovation of the mechanical social organization, which began as massive slavery in the ancient civilizations. About 80% of the population in ancient Greece were slaves.

Institutionalized religion works as instruction manual for the machine. Christianity plays an important role for the indoctrination, by teaching us for thousands of years that life is and a vale of tears full of privation. Later, the evangelical Christians declared the work ethic as new religious doctrine and thus created the basis for capitalistic ideology.[6]

The reward comes after death, if we behave well and obedient during our lifetime. Institutionalized religion has proven to be one of the most effective tools for suppression. Due to almighty belief systems like this, people don't have to be suppressed by brute force; through faith, they will suppress themselves, others and their own children.

Industrial capitalism is the most extreme and by far most destructive form. It combines this form of social organization with actual machines. The humans who are functioning as part of the machine are themselves handling machines all the time. They identify more with their car, their computer, their smartphone and the company they are part of than they identify with other living beings –in-

---

6   Max Weber: "The Protestant Ethic and the Spirit of Capitalism," 1920

cluding humans. The ongoing extinction of insects and songbirds doesn't lead to an uproar. But driving restrictions due to increasing air pollution do. The human parts of the machine can't imagine a life without cars and other machines; the machine belongs to them as they belong to it, and they are absolutely loyal.

Neither the machine nor its parts are intelligent or know any kind of morality. It is not intelligent to poison the air we need to breathe, the water we need to drink, the soil we need to grow food, and even the food itself. Pesticides and Herbicides are weapons of war. Where is the movement for peace?

People who strike, fight for better working conditions or against cutbacks of jobs are already perfectly oiled gears of the machine. They have been born and raised as its parts, and their perception has very restricted limits. They don't know any real freedom. As part of a machine, you don't need to think, but to function. The gainful employment, the profession, is an important part of individual identity.

If humans exist as parts of a machine, they forget how to be responsible for their own lives and the lives of their children. This is why so few people are resisting against the destruction of the planet. The liability for the machine is never carried by its parts. It's a strictly hierarchical system, and the responsibility is always up in the hierarchy.

A machine has no empathy. Applied organized violence is part of its function.

"The West won the world not by the superiority of its ideas or values or religion [...] but rather

This form of social organization made it possible for Europeans to conquer almost the whole world. The machine-like functioning of European society made the brutal extinction of most of life on the American continent possible. Propaganda and rationalizations, like the doctrine of *Manifest Destiny*, served as instruction manuals.

Needless to say that the Third Reich, with the industrial mass extermination of unwanted human beings, worked according to the principles of the megamachine. The IG Farben knew what their Zyclon B would be used for.

For the few people who are still able to think and feel, this culture is long since a dystopian nightmare. For the indoctrinated, this nightmare is the bare reality.

Our culture is based on institutionalized lies that have been erected as barriers to truth. One of the most obvious and thus most propagated lies is that we can have industrial civilization *and* a living planet. The bare truth is that we have to decide. As things stand, most people in our culture made their choice in favor of the megamachine and against a living planet.

After all, humans are animals. The wild packs of wolves, the enemies of civilization, have been exterminated nearly everywhere; nowadays, all that is left are state-owned, domesticated dogs. Dogs can be raised to be the most loving and caring creatures, like guide-dogs who take care of blind humans, with a highly developed social competence. But they can also be conditioned to become terrible monsters, like the Spanish conquistadors with their fighting dogs, fed with butchered Indian children.

Violence has always been the most effective tool of our civilization.

CALL ME CRAZY:
BABYLON APOCALYPSE

Call me crazy, but I spent the last evening sitting in my garden and telling the first toad I met this year what I do and why. I told her about Deep Green Resistance, about the destruction of the natural world by our culture, and I asked her to tell me how she and her kind perceive all this.

I don't know if I understood her correctly, but what I heard was:

"Well, too many of us are dying. We know that some of you are trying to help us. That's not enough. It has to stop."

It doesn't matter if I'm projecting or not. The toad is right.

She wasn't shy, she sat quietly right next to me, moved a little bit every now and then, and looked at me with beautiful, red, serious eyes.

I regularly go to the wildest places that still exist here and listen to nature. I see different kinds of insects, wild bees, bumblebees, mosquitoes, beetles, a few dragonflies. I see – mostly hear – birds, but I can only distinguish about five or six species. I love the call of the codger when it gets dark.

I know that the stag beetles[7] come out of the ground at the beginning of June, where they have lived for three years as increasingly fattening grubs, to fly with a huge hum into the summer forest, where they will live exclusively from the sap of the rare old oaks their females prepare, since the males cannot bite the bark because of their huge antlers. Every June, I wait in my garden to welcome them. Towards the end of the summer they carry out their ecstatic fights and mating rituals, until after spending only three months as Europe's most giant beetles, they die and serve hungry birds as autumn delicacy.

I see squirrels, bats, toads, grass frogs and spotted salamanders. Sometimes I meet bigger animals: Wild boars, badgers, foxes, deer, but they usually flee quickly.

The European bison or wisent, that used to inhabit this forest, I only know from the zoo. But even the ones that are forced to live in captivity are gigantic, beautiful, trusting and kind. They look at me with loving eyes, each of them asking the same question:

---

7   See cover of this book

Twice in my life I've seen a snake. The first encounter was a European adder, many years ago in a village in the Odenwald (the forest where I live). The second one was a giant garter snake in my garden a few months ago. She (or he) was enjoying the sun, lying on a large oak tree that recently had been killed by a storm.

After this encounter, I wanted to learn more about them. I read that garter snakes were treated as house snakes and considered holy animals that bring happiness and blessing. The garter snake was worshipped by numerous European peoples until the late Middle Ages and appears in many myths. People fed garter snakes milk, just as the Indian villagers do in Rudyard Kipling's Jungle Book with their holy village cobra.

Today, you are very lucky if you see a garter snake once in your life.

It's getting dark. I look at the stars and the full moon. I speak to them and all the animals, plants and living beings around me. I tell them what I do and why, and I say prayers. I declare my loyalty. I tell them that I am one of them and that I will do everything in my power to help them. They're my relatives.

I'm asking them to tell me the most important things I can do for them. I tell them that I love them.

The toad is still sitting next to me. She (or he) looks at me, lets me take a photo and politely waits until I'm done talking to her. Then she slowly trots towards the pond I have build for her kind to inhabit.

Like thousands times before, I walk the way from my garden to my small apartment in the city. Like thousands times before, I look down over the Neckar River to see Babylon. I fear Babylon. I'm terrified of Babylon.

The Neckar River once was called Germany's wildest river, but it has been raped for at least 2000 years, since the Roman invaders drained parts of it to build the old bridge, which is still in place today. Nowadays, the River essentially serves as a road for the many freighters that are desperately trying to satisfy the insatiable hunger of Babylon. Like the Rhine, it had been full of salmon in the past, but this was so long ago that no human people can remember. I'm sure some of the trees still know.

During the last two years beavers return, after being absent for about 150 years. There are supposed to be about three thousand of them again in Baden-Württemberg. The state government considers killing about half of them because they are allegedly damaging trees.

The natural world is full of wisdom. So often I've sat here or there, listening, speaking, praying. The river, the forest and all the creatures who still live here speak different languages and have different messages. They taught me a lot, and I have a lot more to learn. But in one thing they all agree:

It has to stop. Babylon Apocalypse.

FAITH

Reality by Eran Fowler

The most basic commandment of our culture:

Thou shalt pretend there is nothing wrong.

Indigenous cultures, uncivilized societies that did not build cities and lived as hunters and gatherers or small scale subsistence farmers, were land-based cultures. Their livelihoods were based on the land and the ecosystems.

Our culture –in the broadest sense civilization, in the narrower sense western, more recently industrial civilization– is based on faith. In terms of livelihoods, our culture is no longer based solely on the exploitation of its land base, but on the hyper-exploitation of almost all parts of the world, including the oceans.

The people of our culture do not live in the real physical world. With their cities they have built their own world, and with their beliefs their own artificial reality. They have sealed themselves off from the real world and the truth. Our culture is characterized by an increasingly complex technology. People are proud of it, identify with it and trust technology with an almost unshakable faith. Last but not least, they regard technology as synonymous with progress. Cultures without complex technology have for our culture about as much value as ecosystems. They are exploited, assimilated, "developed", and ultimately destroyed.

Our culture is based on faith, because only with strong belief systems, coupled with the corresponding propaganda machinery, can a potentially volatile mass like our modern society with its unprecedented number of people be managed, controlled and kept reasonably stable. Mass propaganda has always been of great importance for civilization. From the invention of writing to book printing, newspapers, mail, telegraphy, telephone, fax, radio, television and the Internet; mobile phones and smartphones; to social media, that gives us the illusion of contact with other people, while in reality we are sitting lonely in front of the screen of a machine. Technology is never neutral. Our form of technology is not so much a sign of a particularly advanced culture but a necessary instrument with which those in power keep us under control. The current IT technology with its screen culture and digital hallucinations is the most effective opium for the masses ever invented, and at the same time the most perfect mass surveillance apparatus ever invented.

We have no culture and we have no society.

Although I use these terms for lack of alternatives, our form of society is actually a kind of anti-culture, that destroys any form of original culture and community. A culture would be a set of social rules, values and norms, aimed at organizing a stable and sustainable society. Essentially, *culture* regulates the relationship between human and non-human beings, i.e. the interaction with the land base, as well as the relationships between humans themselves.

The current form of liberalism, capitalism, consumerism, individualism, techno cult and popculture neither knows rules for a meaningful interaction with the land base, nor for the people between themselves. The only rule is the often unspoken, but very strong hierarchy with money as a synonym for power. Money has no value in itself. Yet for most people, money is like a religious fetish for which they do almost everything.

The beliefs of our culture have direct and profound effects on the real world, and my own life. Why do you pay rent? I pay rent because I know that if I didn't, ultimately the police would force me out of my apartment and I'd be homeless. So I pay rent because I have to bow to structural violence. That the landlord owns my apartment and I have to pay for the right to live here is not based on any natural or physical laws, but is a purely social convention. It only works because the majority of the population believes in the right of the owners to exploit those who don't own. In fact I have to work for my landlord, for the only purpose of making him even richer than he already is.

Many of the beliefs on which our culture is based are not particularly credible in themselves and have a quasi-religious character, so the people of our culture must be indoctrinated from an early age. Without permanent indoctrination, our "culture" would immediately fall apart. That is why those in power were so afraid of the 60's hippie culture and drugs like cannabis and LSD: because they are able, in a sense, to resolve social conditioning. But obviously that wasn't enough.

Our economic system is based on the belief in infinite growth on a finite planet. We act on the belief that we can make infinite use of finite fossil fuels. We believe that our transport system is more important than our breathing air, and we act as if a transport system based on fossil fuels and poisoning our air will last forever. We believe in infinite technological progress, and consistently ignore the dramatic effects this belief has on the real world. We believe that we can destroy not only the climate and the oceans, but practically the whole planet and still live on it. We actually know better; yet we –or rather those in power– act according to this faith. And we have been so polite to believe that those in power have the right to diligently destroy our future and the future of our children in order to increase their wealth.

Almost all the beliefs our "culture" is based on are bare lies and not even particularly credible. Out of these lies, the credulous people of our "culture" assemble their small, cozy, intact worlds, which they vehemently defend against the truth. Those who have a glimpse of the fact that not everything is all right will build even more defenses, choosing between New Age esoteric, the myth of the hundredth monkey, the hope of a collective paradigm shift, the belief in digital man as the consciousness of the universe, the golden age etc., in order not to have to see the truth. Here too, the more absurd the faith, the more fervently it is believed and defended against all evidence.

It is no exaggeration to state that this culture is patho-
logically insane. Our self-perception as "culture" is the
self-perception of a madman. We believe that we are the
most developed culture that ever existed and the cultures before us were primitive and regressive. Therefore,
we also believe that it is justified to brutally eradicate
"primitive" indigenous cultures all over the world.
Progress has its price and you can't make an omelet
without breaking eggs. Racism, that is the belief that a
"race" of people (usually those with the lighter skin) are
better, smarter, more progressive, stronger, higher developed than others – along with a distorted version of
Darwin's theory of evolution, the idea of the survival of
the fittest, that applied to human societies forms the ideology of social Darwinism – has created a justification
that has already proven itself in numerous genocides.
Racism naturally refers to beings of other species (we do
not use the term here, although it would be much more
appropriate, since they actually *are* different races). My
point is that indigenous peoples, just like wolves, bison,
salmon, bears, lynxes, whales, gorillas and many other
creatures, have been and continue to be victims of the
Holocaust. And all this is based on the belief that we, as
the crown of creation, have the right to eradicate all others and thus deny them the right to live.

---

*"In order for us to maintain our way of living, we
must, in a broad sense, tell lies to each other,
and especially to ourselves. It is not necessary
that the lies be particularly believable. The lies
act as barriers to truth. These barriers to truth
are necessary because without them many de-
plorable acts would become impossibilities.*

It is actually not difficult to see that our culture is based on violence and destroys all life on this planet. All we have to do is to take off the numerous cultural eyeglasses that guide our perception. Then we will lose faith in all these lies and realize the truth. This automatically puts us outside our "culture" and we cannot go back, because we have recognized it and all the lies for what they really are. Only from the outside do we see our civilization as the terrible monster that consumes and destroys all living things. What remains is solely the faith in Mother Earth and the land base you live on. And that makes sense, because behind all of these collective hallucinations, it is still Mother Earth who keeps us alive. Nature has produced an incredible variety of creatures and will continue to do so if we only let her. So it is the moral duty of every person who no longer identifies with this culture but with the real world, to defend life on the planet against the monster that is civilization.

---

[8]   A Language older than Words, p.2

SOFT POWER

Painting by Kaipo, age 4

"Since the beginning of history, attempts have been made to develop power techniques with which our moral sensitivities can be undermined, so to speak, which activate less resistance in the people. These power techniques are now often referred to as soft power. Soft power is the full range of techniques to manipulate public opinion. Intermediaries for these forms of exercising power are supported by foundations, think tanks, elite networks and lobby groups — in particular private and public media, schools and the entire education and training sector as well as the cultural industry. The effects of soft power techniques are largely invisible to the public, so

Along with destroying livelihoods and community, one of the most important things our "culture" needs to do to function is the destruction of the self. Because if our very selfs wouldn't have been destroyed, we wouldn't put up with any of this shit. We wouldn't go to work to sell eight hours or even more of our lifetime each day. We wouldn't let our world be destroyed by rich, pathological, insane men. We wouldn't inflict daily violence, even if oftentimes in a quite "soft" form, on our own children.

Of course, the destruction of the self is a very long and painful process, and therefore has to start at an early age. Rainer Mausfeld, professor of psychology and cognition research, stated that the term competence (or skill) is one of the most ideological inflicted terms of our time. "The question those in power have been asking," Mausfeld says, "is 'how do we disassemble the self of the individual into a bundle of skills.'" He also states that "school is the most important soft power instrument of the state."

After all, what children learn in school are skills and competences; at the very best they would learn some form of social competence. What they don't learn is to be a human being, to evolve, to think, to feel, to just be.

This concerns me a lot, because I'm the father of a little loving sunshine named Leonard, who will start attending school this summer.

When Leo started going to kindergarten, for me that started a process of remembering my own early childhood. I remembered how much I hated kindergarten as well as school, and it got me thinking about these forms of soft power.

Leo's kindergarten is indeed a very good one. It is one of the famous German "forest kindergartens," which means that the kids will be outside in the forest all day. Still, we had to go through what they call *acclimatization phase*, because a child of three has to be accustomed to being left alone by its parents. During the two weeks of this phase, one of us had to stay with our son at the kindergarten, leaving every now and then for a while to get him used to being without us.

So often I have seen little children cry, when his or her mother would hand him or her over to one of the preschool teachers and leave.

"Don't go mom, don't leave me!" the little ones would scream in sheer panic. "I'm so sorry my little darling, I have to go to work" was the usual answer.

I live in a pretty decent social environment. Most of the middle-class people here are kind and gentle; they love their kids and care for them. Some of them even told me that it breaks their heart to leave them. But they have been conditioned –like all of us– to believe that this is *the way things are*.

One time a child, whose mom had just left with the usual explanation, cried and just wouldn't stop. Ian, who was at that time the oldest boy in kindergarten because he hasn't been considered "ready" for school (seriously, who is?), commented with one of the smartest lines I've ever heard:

> *"We have to go to kindergarten because they have to go to work; If they don't work, they won't earn money; without money, they can't buy groceries, and we'll have to starve; starvation is worse than kindergarten."*

That morning I went home and cried. Seven year old Ian had just covered most of the internal violence of our culture in one sentence with a few semicolons.

Today, I had to wake Leo early at 6:00 AM because I needed to bring him to his mom who would drive him to kindergarten. He hates to be woken up as much as I did as a kid and still do. He was crying and resisting a lot. I hate it when I have to do this, because I know I'm inflicting a "soft" form of violence on him.

I love the quote by Smohalla, the Wanapum dreamer-prophet:

> *"My young men shall never work, men who work cannot dream; and wisdom comes to us in dreams."*

I indeed believe that it is very unhealthy to be woken up early on a regular basis, because natural cycles of sleeping and dreaming are disturbed. That most of us have to get up early from an early age on, for kindergarten, school and later work, is very bad for our mental health and therefore must be considered as part of the destruction of the self that our "culture" is inflicting on us.

Usually, I wake him for kindergarten as late as possible. With everybody busy working, there is no community and no kids to play with in the neighborhood. This is the reason I want him to attend, because kindergarten is the only chance for him to regularly get in contact with other kids and gain some social competence.

We've had some meetings at the elementary school he'll attend. I went there with him, and we stood with a bunch of kids from different kindergartens waiting for the teacher, school kids playing around us. "Class 2b, to the classroom!" a teacher shouted. Immediately, about 25 children would run after her. It is amazing, I thought, how they are conditioned at a very young age to follow military-style orders.

Our teacher came and called us to follow her to the gym. At the door, she took Leo's hand, smiled at me and said: "Daddy is going to wait outside." While everybody else went in, I was the only one who had to stay in the cold schoolyard. After a short startling moment I understood. I'd been the only parent, while all others where preschool teachers.

The system needs to separate us very early, to destroy the strongest bonds of relationships and make us weak and compliant. Of course, most of the teachers are nice and well-meaning people, at least at the elementary school near where I live. But they've gone through the very same process of conditioning. They learned that *the most important thing is to follow orders*. And that is what they do. Especially here in Germany, we should know that this in itself is very, very dangerous.

It terrifies me.

"Indian children are never alone. They are always surrounded by grandparents, uncles, cousins, relatives of all kinds, who fondle the kids, sing to them, tell them stories. If the parents go someplace, the kids go along."
John (Fire) Lame Deer

Schools have been used in the US in a systematic and fierce way to destroy the kind of community Lame Deer describes. Of course, school has been much harder for them then it is for us civilized people. One reason for this is racism, another the systematic destruction of their native cultures and languages, that was largely done through school. But it is also because they just weren't used to it. That time, they still knew how freedom and genuine community feels like. They still had something that we've lost long ago.

"I see men assassinated around me every day. I walk through rooms of the dead, streets of the dead, cities of the dead; men without eyes, men without voices; men with manufactured feelings and standard reactions; men with newspaper brains, television souls and high school ideas."
Charles Bukowski

I've been asking myself why school is taking so long. I attended school for 12 painful years and seriously, most of the time was wasted. Learning to read and write is not that hard; neither is learning some basic math. There are thousands of great books out there that cover much more than the things they teach you in school. Any average intelligent person could prepare for graduation in one or two years.

So, why all the wasted time?

Because the function of the school system is, first and foremost, to condition us with the experience that our lifetime doesn't belong to us, but to a system. We have to be conditioned to sell eight hours or even more of our lifetime each day. We have to be conditioned, and broken, to identify with the company we work for, instead of identifying with a community of family and friends, or even the landbase we live on and the larger community of our nonhuman relatives.

This is why they destroy all of it. The community, the land, and even the self.

Otherwise, we'd never put up with any of that shit. We'd resist, just like the American Indians did, until death.

FREEDOM

"Capitalism reaches fulfillment when it sells communism as a commodity. Communism as a commodity spells the end of revolution."
Byung-Chul Han

I'm a permaculturalist. And I became a permie in the first place because I wanted to break free from this culture.

To me, permaculture was and still is highly political.

is one of my favorite Bill Mollison quotes. After all, what freedom can we have without subsistence, without having control over our most basic resources, our own food?

said Native American activist John Mohawk.

I've been so ardent and naive. I thought that the permaculture approach is so ingenious that it would become a mass-movement, indeed a quiet and peaceful revolution. It would free us from being dependent on the digital food they sell us in grocery stores nowadays and from the wage economy at the same time, because we would build small, local food cooperatives that would all *share the surplus*.

Unfortunately, time and experience shows that it's not that easy.

One of my permaculture teachers, who taught me the concept of the food forest, often said:

He also articulated a very strange notion about the future:

Attendants hung on his lips when he said that, and while everybody else was amazed by this perspective of a golden future, I sat quietly, stunned.

I knew in my heart that he was wrong, but couldn't articulate a sufficient answer to his statements back then.

But they made me angry. How can one say that "we have all the freedoms we want," while the air we need to breathe is being polluted, the greatest mass extinction in planetary history is happening, the climate is being destroyed, the oceans are vacuumed and filled with toxic garbage, in short: when the most basic functions of our planet to support life are being destroyed?

What about the freedom of having breathable air? What about the freedom of having a livable planet? What about the freedom of having a future?

I've given a lot of thought to his statements ever since, because they seem so appealing to many people. The Earth never supported more than 2 billion humans, until Fritz Haber and Robert Bosch indeed broke the planetary boundaries with the invention of the Haber-Bosch process. Nowadays, we are hopelessly overpopulated. So the number of 10 billion is purely random and nothing but magical thinking. The notion of Internet technology and humans as the consciousness of the planet is nothing more than a new fashion of the good old ideology of humans as the crown of creation. What about nature in this fantasy? With 10 billion (industrial) humans, there will hardly be anything left.

Everybody with a sane mind and a little understanding — especially a permie — should know that the trees, the fungi, the soil, the air, the water, the animals and so on, in short what we call *nature*, indeed *is* the consciousness of planet earth. Apparently, the *manifest destiny* of the technocrats is to eradicate what they perceive as primitive, raw, red in tooth and claw, wild and uncontrollable, and to replace nature with a "better" system of human technology.

Deconstructing that was the easy part. The hard part is his statement about freedom. With all this in mind, the primary question is: what does *freedom* mean for someone like him?

A guy I know, who was lucky enough to hear Noam Chomsky speak live, told me that in the discussion after somebody asked the usual question:

"What can we do about it?"

Chomsky responded that this is a strange question. People from so-called developing countries would never ask such a question, instead they would tell him in which form of resistance they already engage. Apparently, third-world-people still have a clearer sense for suppression and cultures of resistance.

"We should rather ask what we can't do"

Chomsky said.

When I attended a talk by Rainer Mausfeld, of course someone asked the very same question. Mausfeld stated that this question shows how well the *soft power tech-*

niques he'd been describing work. We can't even *imag-ine* any form of resistance.

For more than a century, the analysis of the political left has been very clear: The suppression and exploitation of the poor (working class) by the rich (owning class), that is the very basis of capitalism, can only be solved by organized class struggle to come from the working class. This concept isn't hard to understand. It is classic Marxism. But somehow the ruling class has managed to completely eradicate it from the proletarian minds.

I've come across a lot more of what I like to call liberal lifestyle-activists. I understood that most permies chose permaculture not because they want a revolution (like I did), but because they want a more sustainable lifestyle for themselves. They believe that they are free, because they perceive their individualism and their freedom of choice as the greatest freedom, the greatest achievement of modernity. Being part of any group, class or movement is perceived as regressive. The notion of class struggle is *so yesterday.*

At the same time, they're usually educated people and they know that a lot of things are going badly wrong. But as liberals who are taking power out of the equation, and individualists lacking any concept of social group our class, they must take it all on themselves.

"It is all of us who are causing the destruction"

they'd say.

As a result, the only thinkable form of political action are personal consumer choices. Buy organic soap and feel better.

A great example of this are vegans. No doubt that factory farming is horrible and has to stop. But as a lifestyle-activist, all you can do about it is to stop consuming meat. In your world view, the problem can only be solved by everybody stopping eating meat.

For liberal lifestyle-activists, "having all the freedoms we want" can only mean the freedom to consume (or not consume) whatever we want, whenever we want, in any quality and quantity we want. This is the kind of "freedom" with which capitalism has hijacked us. If we can afford it, of course. But within neoliberal capitalist ideology, there is no such thing as a suppressed class. The poor are poor because they don't work hard enough, or they are simply to stupid to sell themselves well enough.

"Neoliberalism turns the oppressed worker into a free contractor, an entrepreneur of the self. Today, everyone is a self-exploiting worker in their own enterprise. Every individual is master and slave in one. This also means that class struggle has become an internal struggle with oneself. Today, anyone who fails to succeed blames themselves and feels ashamed. People see themselves, not society, as the problem."
Byung-Chul Han[9]

For radicals, the question remains: Without the possibility of mass movements, how do we stop the destruction of the planet that is our only home?

---

9   https://www.opendemocracy.net/transformation/byung-chul-han/why-revolution-is-no-longer-possible

For a new generation of serious activists who are tired of all that shit and ready to take action, DGR has the Decisive Ecological Warfare[10] strategy.

---

10 http://deepgreenresistance.org/deep-green-resistance-strategy/decisive-ecological-warfare

LETTER TO MY
MIDDLE CLASS FRIENDS

Dear J.,

Congratulations on your new job!

To be honest, I've never understood how people like you can do practically anything for their job, while the whole world around us is burning.

This is not a criticism of your person, but only my attempt to better understand your way of life.

I know you do have some understanding that our entire culture is based on violence and exploitation and destroys all life on the planet. Nevertheless, you do everything to be a functioning part of the machine and to live a "normal" western life.

It must be because we have been socialized in completely different ways. You belong to the wealthy middle class, and they are doing everything to maintain the status quo.

It must be because they are more separated from the physical world, from the real world, than I am. They have something I never had, namely a world of their own.

It is this bubble of their middle class status that still guarantees them many privileges. They can afford flights and holidays, they have the power and status to travel to many places in the world, and they always have enough money. The bubble gives them a false sense of security through privileges I've never known. They live within this bubble and do not perceive themselves as part of the real physical world around them.

For me, it always was about whether we could afford another pack of noodles or potatoes at the end of the month, or whether we could pay the rent, so we wouldn't get kicked out of the apartment. The apartment that was owned by someone from the middle class, to whom this entitlement and the rent he exploited from us gave exactly this deceptive security.

Because they live in their own bubble of privileges and "security" and not in the real physical world, the destruction, which frightens me terribly, doesn't frighten them as much, or at least can be accepted much better because, in their perception, it somehow happens outside their own sphere.

I've been an outsider from the beginning, I've always lived on the edge. The narratives and symbols of this culture have never made any sense to me, because I have seen and experienced relative poverty, oppression and exploitation from the beginning. The pictures of slaughtered whales and the sea of blood I saw in Greenpeace magazines at the age of six stuck in my head forever.

For me, there has never been a status of comfortable "normality." I've tried for a while to adapt, to become "normal," but I just couldn't. I know by now that normality can never exist within this culture based on violence and exploitation. At least not for me.

But strangely enough – and this is exactly what I find so difficult to understand – the narratives and symbols of this culture still make sense to you affluent middle class, even though you are educated and know that the world is on fire. Somehow you still manage to stay within the system and serve it. And somehow you guys are doing pretty well.

I wonder what it takes to break your "normality," to get you out of your comfort zone and do things that are not "normal."

The fact that 90% of fish in the oceans have disappeared is not enough. The biggest mass extinction in the history of the planet is not enough. The imminent threat of climate change to all life on planet earth is not enough.

I can't help myself, but it keeps me thinking of our recent history, when the good German citizens did everything to preserve "normality." About 1000 concentration camps in the German Reich and the occupied areas, in which millions of people were systematically industrially slaughtered, were not enough to get the middle class out of their comfort zone. The (presumably middle class) SS commander in the concentration camp was a loving family man in his spare time.

But the thing is, if the planet is destroyed, it will affect you too. You too will lose your privileges, because when the planet is destroyed, *all of us lose everything*.

You too are dependent on clean air, clean drinking water and halfway decent food. This is the absolute truth, even if all other "truths" around us (propaganda, ideology, you name it...) are extremely flexible and can be adapted to the prevailing political system.

I wish you all the best and a good life inside your bubble. Perhaps we'll meet some day in hell, when the dystopian nightmare I already live in has destroyed your privileges and your lives too.

Love & Rage,

Bo

APOCALYPTO

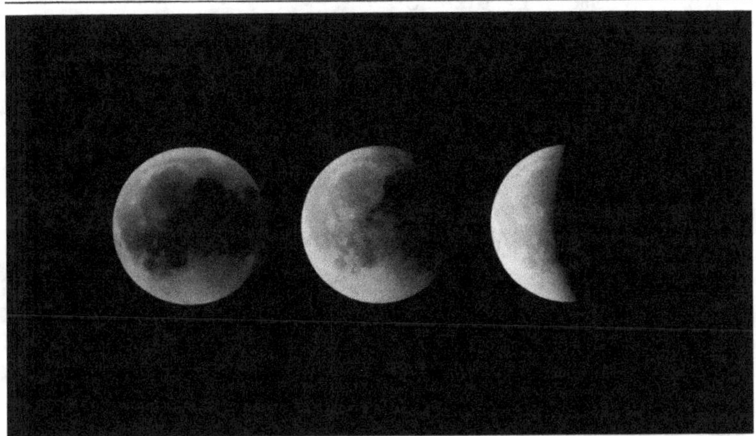

It is very difficult for me to live in this culture.

I just can't psychologically survive in the high performance society, where everyone is passionately exploiting themselves while all life on this planet is being destroyed.

I have severe depression and anxiety disorders and I have to take good care of myself to be able to take care of my son.

It is very difficult for people who have never experienced poverty to understand what poverty means. The constant nagging fear. The permanent stress and psychological terror of state authorities on which you are dependent, that harass you and try to keep you small and oppressed.

Now they want me to work underpaid, shitty jobs again. I already had a stroke not long ago. I can't do these jobs, and I can't stand the pressure.

I live in the age of the greatest mass extinction in 65 million years. And the cause of this mass extinction is our glorious western civilization.

Empire.

Indeed, almost all imperial forces have joined into one: The West.

"In the last eighteen months, the greatest build-up of military forces since World War Two — led by the United States — is taking place along Russia's western frontier... The United States is encircling China with a network of bases, with ballistic missiles, battle groups, nuclear-armed bombers..."
John Pilger[11]

Looks like the West is encircling the strongest probable future enemies, preparing for war.

Full spectrum dominance.

The understanding of the fact that this culture is always at war and will indeed kill all life on planet earth made me shift my loyalty and become an activist. My loyalty does not belong to empire and industrial capitalism. My loyalty belongs to the suppressed, the poor, the dying planet.

Where are you when we need people to take responsibility for our fellow creatures, human and nonhuman, and defend them? Always working on your professional self-fulfillment, performing until you burn out.

---

11   http://www.free21.org/a-world-war-has-begun-break-the-silence/?lang=en

Do you distract yourself so manically with your work, so you don't have to see what is happening around us? That the insects disappear, the songbirds disappear, the masses impoverish?

That the West is already bombing the near and middle east to ashes and dust and prepares for more, while you try to overtake yourself, become faster and better, without even stopping once to understand the obvious fact that this system is heading for collapse?

Instead you wonder where all the refugees come from. (Of course they come for a share of the cake of our western wealth, they might even try to take your precious job! You better join one of the aspiring right-wing movements.)

Imperialism creates the illusion of wealth as far as the masses are concerned. It usually serves to hide the fact that the ruling classes are gobbling up the natural resources of the home territory in an improvident manner and are otherwise utilizing the national wealth largely for their own purposes. Eventually the general public is called upon to pay for all of this, frequently after the military machine can no longer maintain external aggression.
Jack Forbes

Capitalism 2.0 comes with a like-button and a smiling emoji, and it will always tell you that *everything is fine.*

Capitalism is exploitation, but Neoliberalism is the smart self-exploitation of the alienated and indoctrinated individual. Exploitation on steroids.

Indoctrination is cheaper and more efficient than violence. It is thus called "Soft Power." It works with research-based psycho-politics and the smart manipulation of human feelings and desires.

Capitalism creates an exploited class of workers that will probably organize and resist (as it did many times).

Neoliberalism creates a population of totally alienated and indoctrinated machine-like zombies, who suppress their own humanity. Each individual a perfect slave, with a software programmed in its brain. Owner Inside®.

Zombie Apocalypse.

You might already be a zombie, living in your middle class-bubble or your digital hallucination, but I am still a human being, sensitive as a frightened child, with a healthy portion of empathy and love. I'm trying to live awake and conscious in this real, physical world, and what I see is mass extinction, ecological catastrophe and imperialist wars. Trauma.

Facing the truth isn't easy. I carry a trauma with me from reading *A Short Account of the Destruction of the Indies* by Bartolome de Las Casas.

I carry a trauma with me from reading Jack Forbes' *Columbus and other cannibals* and *Only Approved Indians.* He writes:

"If a creature learns to completely accept captivity or slavery, if they erase all thoughts of freedom, they can suppress the pain. But if one wants to be free, one has to face the pain; one has to agonize, to suffer, through all of the terror."

That's where you are. Completely accepting captivity and slavery, driving out the pain.

That's where I am. Going through all the terror. Trying to free myself (and the world) of this culture.

I carry a trauma with me from reading Derrick Jensen's *Endgame*. And I carry a deep trauma with me from seeing that he is right, from seeing my fellow beings and relatives disappear, the insects, the birds, the amphibians, all of my beloved nature in rapid decline, my frame of reverence destroyed.

I most certainly carry a lot of trauma with me from my parents and grandparents, since I was born only 34 years after World War II. I certainly carry a trauma from watching all the documentaries and from visiting the concentration camp in Dachau.

You do not understand my language. I can say what I want, but you don't understand. You do not even understand the language "stroke" (red alert; Individual doesn't function anymore within this insane culture).

"Government to medical complex: Repair individual and re-integrate into the machine."

Sorry, doesn't work for me. I'm out.

I need a lot of quiet and peaceful time to deal with all the trauma. I can't just rush through my life and work ever harder to help to accomplish the neoliberal agenda and *make Europe more competitive for the global economy* (that's how the politicians sold it to us; in fact, the rich are getting richer and the poor poorer, as always).

> *"Mental illnesses such as depression or burnout
> are the expression of a deep crisis of freedom.
> They are a pathological sign that today freedom
> often turns into coercion. We think we are free
> today. But in reality we exploit ourselves pas-
> sionately until we collapse...*
>
> *"Neoliberalism is even capable of exploiting free-
> dom itself. The performance society creates
> more productivity than the disciplinary society,
> because it makes excessive use of freedom. It
> doesn't exploit against freedom, but it exploits
> freedom itself. Everything that belongs to prac-
> tices and expressions of freedom, such as emo-
> tion, play and communication, is now exploited.
> It is not efficient to exploit someone against his
> or her will. With the external exploitation, the
> yield is very small. Only self-exploitation, as the
> exploitation of freedom, produces the greatest
> yield. The first stage of burnout syndrome is,
> paradoxically, euphoria. Euphorically I plunge
> into the work. In the end I collapse and slide into
> depression."*
> *Byung-Chul Han[12]*

What will you do when the next economic collapse hits?

What will you do when you loose your job and can't
numb yourself anymore with your work?

Alcohol, drugs, suicide?

---

12   https://www.swr.de/-/id=14631196/property=download/nid=660374/1lz1me7/s
     wr2-wissen-20150111.pdf

Better to face the truth, go through all the terror, declare your loyalty to justice and life on planet earth and
become a revolutionary.

49

PRESERVE AND PROTECT REMAINING UNTOUCHED WILDERNESS

After I wrote the previous article and posted it on facebook, someone posted a video of the positivist permie Matt Powers,[13] a guy who seems to be always smiling and promotes "UNSTOPPABLE ENTHUSIASM"[14] in response.

It made me think, and I articulated my thoughts in this article.

A positivist person like Matt Powers is certainly more successful in this society than a negative person. And yes, I often wish I could be as positive as Matt. I find the positivism in permaculture sometimes refreshing, but

---

13   http://www.thepermaculturestudent.com
14   https://www.booktopia.com.au/unstoppable-enthusiasm-matt-powers/prod9781732187863.html

sometimes, I must confess, I find it frighteningly naive. Don't get me wrong. I love permaculture, and I think that as many people as possible should apply and propagate permaculture. But honestly, if a few activists grow their own food on a few square meters or even a few hectares and build small eco-paradises while the majority of the people in this culture continues to engage in terribly destructive industrial activities, they will have destroyed our world much faster than we, the small handfuls of activists, manage to regenerate nature.

I think it's great that Matt Powers explicitly refers to these two of Mollison's guiding principles:

---

1. Preserve and Protect Remaining Untouched Wilderness
2. Rehabilite Degraded Land

What I love about permies is that many of them have a good understanding of nature. There is an understanding that we desperately need ecological regeneration. And we are proud that we even have viable solutions for climate change – at least in theory. But how do you regenerate hundred million murdered American bison? Gosh, if a permie managed to restore only a herd of 10,000 wild bison and their habitat, this person would forever be my hero.

It's great that permaculture carries the knowledge of how to re-green deserts or regenerate hopelessly overused landscapes, like the Loess Plateau in China. If this culture changed in a way, so that it would use the 69 million dollars *per hour* that are currently spent for the gigantic US military apparatus (and thus to maintain the full spectrum dominance of Empire and to kill, and kill, and kill...), to ecologically regenerate destroyed areas, I would be happy and positive for the rest of my life.

If we are honest, we have to admit that very few permies are committed to the guiding principle of Mollison, to *Preserve and Protect Remaining Untouched Wilderness.* Most Permies are committed to grow their own food on a small scale. The permaculture movement with all its great ethical principles, its knowledge and its positivism is blind to the real problem:

That we are governed by psychopaths who have enormous power and use it to wage a brutal war of annihilation against all life on this planet. And the extent of permaculture activism stands in no relation to the extent of the destruction. To resist, and to resist effectively, would actually be much more important than to cultivate a few small permaculture gardens. But of course – and this is probably the reason why more people in the West engage in permaculture than in resistance (you could also call it *preserving and protecting remaining untouched wilderness*) – resistance is damn difficult and associated with numerous dangers.

As a gardener, you usually don't have to deal with repression by police or military. And what about those people who still live in sustainable societies in so-called developing countries, who already practice something like permaculture (even if they don't use the term), whose livelihoods are destroyed by the West and the monster that feeds us, industrial capitalism? Wouldn't it be our moral duty to stand by them? How can we invoke the ethical principle of *peoplecare* while the West, with industrial capitalism and global trade, destroys small-scale subsistence farming all over the world?

But even within the permaculture movement – at least this applies to Germany – we will not be able to avoid political disputes. At least if we seriously want to establish permaculture as an alternative to the destructive practices of agriculture. In any case, we would need a radical land reform in order to get more land than the few small gardens, backyards and abandoned parking lots that the municipalities sometimes mercifully leave to urban gardening initiatives for temporary use.

As we know, those who own the land usually don't like it if their claim to ownership is questioned. This also applies to the agricultural industry. Land reform will require serious political struggle.

I'll become a positivist the very day I realize that there are more insects and more songbirds this year than the year before. That is all I need to be positive and happy. I don't really care how this happens. But after a sober look, I came to the disillusioning conclusion that it would require the crash of our culture. Because our culture, western civilization, industrial capitalism and global trade, is the cause for the worst mass extinction in the history of the planet.

Permaculture is fantastic. Permaculture is something wonderful. And permaculture can certainly play an important role in saving our planet. But permaculture alone will not be enough. If current trends continue and bees and other insects continue to disappear, this will affect permies as well.

Permies are perhaps those who are – at least theoretically – best prepared for coming droughts. But still, if current trends continue and climate change makes large parts of the world uninhabitable, permaculture, in its current form, can hardly prevent it. And I'm not even mentioning our moral duty to stop the current neo-imperial wars.

All of these are extremely pressing political problems, that cannot be solved by permaculture and gardening alone. But let us not delude ourselves. Positivism often is also a form of denial.

In my permaculture courses I always had a strong focus on the destructiveness of agriculture. I have given long and academic lectures on the ten-thousand year history of destruction. I did this because I wanted to show that we live in an extremely violent culture that is waging a brutal war of annihilation against all life, and to convince people that the permaculture movement could and should actually be a movement for peace. But I noticed that most people do not want to know any of this. They want simple, easy to use, practical solutions for their small gardens.

Building alternatives to our current destructive system is something wonderful and incredibly important. But still, and above all, we need those who take up the fight to *Preserve and Protect Remaining Untouched Wilderness*. We need those who actually stop the murder of our planet.

POLITICAL EDUCATION FOR THE POOR – AN ADVOCACY FOR A NEW POLITICAL AWARENESS

"Coming to a political consciousness is not a painless task. To overcome denial means facing the everyday, normative cruelty of a whole society, a society made up of millions of people who are participating in that cruelty, and if not directly, then as bystanders with benefits. A friend of mine who grew up in extreme poverty recalled becoming politicized during her first year in college, a year of anguish over the simple fact that "there were rich people and there were poor people, and there was a relationship between the two." You may have to face full-on the painful experiences you denied in order to survive, and even the humiliation of your own collusion. But

Strictly speaking, all of my problems, the whole drama of my life and suffering can be summarized in one word: **poverty.**

From birth, it seems to have been my destiny, the element that determines my life the most. I really don't want to see myself as a victim. But I can no longer accept the widespread opinion (one could also call it *dominant ideology*) that everyone is responsible for his or her own destiny; that everyone can make it, if he or she only strives and works hard enough. Because it is simply wrong.

I have tried seriously for many years to gain a foothold in the world of work. I am smart, educated, have a well-groomed appearance, and two academic degrees. But it's not my fault.

My "mistake" was merely to enter the "labour market" shortly after the introduction of Gerhard Schroeder's Agenda 2010 and the associated *Hartz "reforms"*.[16]

What the poor need to understand is that poverty is a political goal, because poverty is a fundamental pillar of capitalism.

---

15 Aric McBay, Lierre Keith and Derrick Jensen (2011): Deep Green Resistance: Stategy to Save the Planet S. 73
16 I'd describe the German *HartzIV*-laws to the English-speaking public merely as a kind of poverty management. To quote Wikipedia: „The unemployment benefit II (colloquially mostly Hartz IV) is the basic security benefit for employable beneficiaries in Germany according to the Second Book of the Social Code (SGB II) (...) However, it can be shortened or completely deleted by permissible sanctions; the subsistence minimum is not paid unconditionally."

Money, at least in theory, is nothing more than a means of exchange. But as it is used in reality, it is an ideological instrument of power with a quasi-religious character, which is used with increasing brutality.

As Max Wilbert writes in a recent interview:[17]

> *"The world today is being run by people who believe in money as a god. They're insane, but they have vast power, and they're using that power in the real world. That's the physical manifestation of their violent, corrupt ideology."*

In his book *Endgame*, the writer Derrick Jensen radically deconstructs the "religion" of money. He writes:

> *"There are no rich people in the world, and there are no poor people. There are just people. The rich may have lots of pieces of green paper that many pretend are worth something—or their presumed riches may be even more abstract: numbers on hard drives at banks — and the poor may not. These "rich" claim they own land, and the "poor" are often denied the right to make that same claim. A primary purpose of the police is to enforce the delusions of those with lots of pieces of green paper. Those without the green papers generally buy into these delusions almost as quickly and completely as those with. These delusions carry with them extreme consequences in the real world."[18]*

---

17   https://dgrnewsservice.org/resistance/strategy/towards-a-revolutionary-ecology-an-interview-with-max-wilbert/
18   Derrick Jensen (2006) Endgame Vol 1: The Problem of Civilization p. XI

Money is power. Poverty is an immaterial prison. And the Hartz-laws, with the contemptuous ideology and systematic agitation (classism) behind them, are an immaterial concentration camp.

Welcome to fascism 2.0, the smart fascism of the 21st century.

First of all: I am aware that the comparison with the concentration camps is sensitive. In no way do I want to trivialize the horror of the physical Nazi concentration camps. Under no circumstances should this comparison be understood as a disregard for the suffering of the victims and their descendants.

I am talking about an *immaterial concentration camp,* to make it clear that this time, it's mainly *ideological walls* in which the inmates are held prisoner.

This ideology, however, has some functional parallels with the real concentration camps. And these practices have been incorporated into a legal framework in German legislation, namely the SGB II, colloquially called Hartz Laws.

Expropriation: Whoever ends up in the immaterial concentration camp HartzIV is systematically expropriated. He/she is forced to sell any "usable property", including saved retirement provisions. Without Newspeech, one could also simply say they are robbed.

Disenfranchisement: Rights enshrined in the German Basic Law, such as the right to freedom of movement and free choice of occupation, no longer apply.

"HartzIV is an open prison system"

---

says entrepreneur Götz Werner. In fact, HartzIV recipients are subject to the so-called "Accessibility Order", that means they must be reachable at any time by letter post in order to be able to come to the authority the next day, to immediately be available for a job offer.

Forced labour: HartzIV recipients must accept any "reasonable work" under threat of sanctions. Journalist Susan Bonath writes about this:

> *"The unemployed, for example, were assigned to do clean-up work or collect garbage in cities, they had to maintain green spaces and monuments or to read aloud in nursing homes. All models had and have one thing in common: those affected work at extremely low wages, from which they alone cannot live. Compulsory work models for outsourced workers are not inventions of modern capitalists. Let us recall the workhouses, whose history stretches from the early modern period to the industrial age. The German fascists established the Reich Labour Service. The aim of those in power behind it is clear: they wanted to make the unemployment that was increasingly produced in times of crisis invisible and – more or less brutally – to prevent those affected through employment from thinking about their situation."[19]*

There have been cases where women have been advised by the authorities to prostitute themselves, because –

---

19   https://www.rubikon.news/artikel/der-andere-krieg (translated from German)

also thanks to Gerhard Schröder – this is now nothing more than a legal job in the service sector.[20]

Demoralization: Recipients are regularly summoned to appointments under threat of sanctions and interrogated like criminals, furthermore demoralized with the apportionment of blame and shame to be "difficult to mediate". The institutions are operating a perfidious psycho-terror in order to scare their victims (called "customers" in neoliberal Newspeech), and systematically demoralize them. With the words of anti-HartzIV activist Manfred Bartl:

> *"At no point is it really about 'the human being', but about either breaking him or her and/or making him or her identify with his ongoing oppression. But where this succeeds, nobody resists against this regime any more, because then everyone believes it: I am obviously to blame myself, I have experienced it often enough in the meantime... hence the problem of mass unemployment are not the unemployed, who only had to be "improved", as the Hartz IV regime repeatedly circulates, but it's the increasingly inhuman "labour market" on the one hand and the Social Code II, which literally keeps them out, on the other!"[21]*

---

20   "The prostitution law now in force came into being under the red-green government of Gerhard Schröder (SPD) and has been in force since January 2002. It is considered to be one of the most liberal in the world – which earned him the accusation of having made Germany the "brothel of Europe". Since 2002, sex work has no longer been regarded as "immoral", but as a service. Prostitutes have the opportunity to register for health insurance, pension and unemployment insurance. Two years earlier, Sweden had banned prostitution; since then, customers of sex work are criminalized."
https://www.tagesspiegel.de/politik/prostitutionsgesetz-guetesiegel-fuer-bordelle/10334474.htmlie (translated from German)

21   https://www.nachdenkseiten.de/?p=25168 (translated from German)

Exclusion, stigmatization and the creation of a new class of people: Indeed, the entire design of the HartzIV ideological concentration camp aims to create a new class of people in Germany that previously didn't exist in this way. And it aims to keep the new lower class powerless and dependent. Resistance is suffocated from the outset by a perfidious, sophisticated mixture of ideology, class division through systematic propaganda in the corporate media, the greatest possible economic dependence and the permanent fear of those affected through the threat of sanctions.

Philosopher Byung-Chul Han who studies the neoliberal psycho politics comments:

> *"It's madness how scared the Hartz people live here. They are held in this bannoptikum,[22] so that they do not break out of their fear-cell. I know many Hartzer, they are treated like garbage. In one of the richest countries in the world, Germany, people are treated like scum. Dignity is taken away from them. Of course, these people do not protest because they are ashamed. They blame themselves instead of blaming or accusing society. No political action can be expected from this class."[23]*

With the new class, the institutions created by the Hartz laws administer an army of workers who are supplied at

---

22 A *panopticon* is a type of institutional building and a system of control designed by the English philosopher and social theorist Jeremy Bentham in the late 18th century. It is a design where a guard can watch all the prisoners from the middle. The term panopticon is nowadays used as a synonym for the global mass surveillance. A *bannopticon* in this sense is a prison in which the inmates are banned, becoming invisible for the public.

23 Interview Zeit Online: https://www.zeit.de/zeit-wissen/2014/05/byung-chul-han-philosophie-neoliberalismus (translated from German)

the lowest level and who must be available, mobile, and flexible at all times for any kind of work. As such, they exert enormous pressure on those who still have regular jobs. The Agenda 2010 was therefore also an effective instrument for wage dumping and the creation of a new, gigantic low-wage sector, for which Gerhard Schröder received great praise by his colleagues from France and other European countries.

The declared aim of the institutions (Newspeech *Jobcenter*) is to provide the unemployed with jobs that secure their livelihood, that means to get them out of unemployment (and thus out of unemployment statistics) as quickly as possible. However, this goal is nothing more that another of the usual neoliberal lies. In reality, very few people manage to escape from dependence. The authorities thus also administer a large part of the *working poor* who work, but whose wages are below the HartzIV level. They fall out of the official statistics, but remain dependent and under the full control of the authorities, with all the measures mentioned above.

The propaganda often proves to be a self-fulfilling prophecy for the new class in a familiar way: derided as lazy alcoholics, many actually end up as apathetic alcoholics in order to endure their hopeless existence.

This is indeed a contemptuous treatment of a class of people who are no longer worth anything in our culture. They are superfluous, rubbish, rejects, waste. We've seen this before.

It's therefore not surprising that HartzIV recipients have a significantly increased stress level. Physicians know that chronic stress is one of the most common causes of life-threatening cardiovascular disease and strokes.

Those who die of stress and anxiety or end up in the medical-industrial complex are excluded from unemployment statistics. This is how concentration camps work today.

But in smart fascism 2.0, violence is ideologically much better packaged and gets along without its direct physical forms, because direct, physical violence always generates resistance, which the system must suppress or avoid.

The modern ruling class no longer needs to get their hands dirty. Instead, they use what Rainer Mausfeld calls "Soft Power":

"The most important goal is to neutralize the will of the population to change society, or to divert attention to politically irrelevant goals. In order to achieve this in the most robust and consistent way possible, manipulation techniques aim at much more than just political opinions. They aim at a targeted shaping of all aspects that affect our political, social and cultural life, as well as our individual ways of life. To a certain extent, they aim to create a 'new human being' whose social life merges into the role of the politically apathetic consumer. In this sense they are totalitarian, so that the great democracy-theorist Sheldon Wolin rightly speaks of an 'inverted totalitarianism', a new form of totalitarianism that is not perceived by the population as totalitarianism."[24]

---

24 Rainer Mausfeld (2018): Warum schweigen die Lämmer? p. 17f (translated from German)

One cannot understand our society, or rather what is left of it, without realizing that it consists of social groups or classes. Capitalist/neoliberal ideology says that there are no classes or groups, not even society.

"Who is society? There is no such thing!" said the Iron Lady Margaret Thatcher. Within neoliberal ideology, there are only individuals who (must) assert their own interests on the market. Meanwhile, the ideology as promoted by Thatcher has indeed managed to completely atomize what was left of society and to transform it into an aggregate of totally isolated and alienated individuals, competing against each other on the labor market and passionately exploit themselves while those below languishing inside the immaterial prison poverty or the Hartz-concentration camp.

The ideology is deeply hammered into our heads. We have been taught to feel so much shame about our failure that we do not resist. Instead, we submit to these modern forms of slavery and forced labor. The systematic hatred between classes makes it so that the intellectuals and the middle class, who would have the moral duty to show solidarity with the lower classes and to reject such systematic oppression unfortunately are mostly followers and accept the modern concentration camps, just as the good Germans already did in the past. They could have (must have!) got up, back then as well as now, and said: We are not going with that!

Many people (at least in Germany) still tend to regard the legal system and executive authorities as something positive, as institutions created to serve and help the population. In the meantime, neoliberal Newspeak prevails here as well. Laws and authorities are increasingly created and used as instruments of exploitation and op-pression. "Law organizes power", as lawyer Catherine McKinnon puts it.

The social reality of the lower classes, of those impris-oned in poverty or HartzIV, cannot (and shall not) be un-derstood by the upper classes, the well-earning doctors, lawyers, judges and so on, and the middle class, which is being indoctrinated and passionately exploits itself. Therefore these classes are easily accessible to the agita-tion and classism practiced by those in power. There is very little resistance against the mass impoverishment, oppression and systematic exploitation of large sections of the population with the Hartz laws.

As Susan Bonath writes,

"The Macron government in France is also plan-ning massive social cuts. And it wants to spy on the unemployed in a similar way to Germany. Therefore, the Paris Ministry of Labour recently announced, the administrative staff would be in-creased. Instead of 200, 1,000 inspectors will in future be released onto the unemployed. The goal of the agenda of those in power here and there is clear: employees will be muzzled. They should stay still for fear of relegation. The servi-tude of the 21st century sends its greetings."[25]

Before the Macron government could push its "reforms" as far as the Schröder government did in Germany, masses of poor people are already taking to the streets in France and other countries. The yellow warning vests

---

25   https://www.rubikon.news/artikel/der-andere-krieg (translated from German)

they wear are a powerful symbol of a united resistance of the poor and economically detached.

If you currently walk around Heidelberg where I live, a rich and rather elitist university town with a yellow vest, people look at you like a criminal. "Working class", their looks say, "underclass", "dirt".

Before putting on the vest I had unfortunately forgotten that (even symbolic) resistance, which is merely a struggle for our basic rights and livelihoods, is prohibited in the highly conformist German society, which is effectively policing itself by social norms. "Inverted totalitarianism" indeed.

The usual self-righteous, dismissive commentaries of the bourgeoisie on the violence of the insurgents are blind to the inherent forms of systematic economic and structural violence deeply rooted in our social system, against which the poor and economically detached with the yellow vests resist. They do not want to see that our society

---

"is based on a clearly defined and widely accepted yet often unarticulated hierarchy. Violence done by those higher on the hierarchy to those lower is nearly always invisible, that is, unnoticed. When it is noticed, it is fully rationalized. Violence done by those lower on the hierarchy to those higher is unthinkable, and when it does occur is regarded with shock, horror, and the fetishization of the victims."[26]

I just heard from an activist who got a visit from the Criminal Investigation Department *because she had a*

---

26   Derrick Jensen (2006) Endgame Vol 1: The Problem of Civilization p. IX

yellow vest hanging from her balcony. She was told by the police that it is "not okay for someone to show one's political opinion like that".

Welcome to Fascism 2.0. It is time for a global uprising of the poor. Our common goal must be to deprive the rich of their ability to steal from the poor and the powerful of their ability to destroy the planet.

Stand up.

POLITICAL EDUCATION 101

The idea for this article came to me when I heard a man say at a demonstration that he was confused because he didn't know if he was "right" or "left". It therefore seems very important to me to define such seemingly basic political terms as sharply and clearly as possible.

"left" & "right":

The terms "left" and "right" as political terms have their origins in the French Revolution. At the first French National Assemblies, the traditionally "more honorable" seat to the *right* of the President of Parliament was reserved for the nobility, so that the bourgeoisie (the relatively wealthy middle class, or capitalist class in Marxist contexts) sat on the *left*. Therefore, those who want more equality are called "left" until today, while those who want to preserve existing power structures are called "right".

Some definitions:

"By 'left' we mean a commitment to social change towards greater equality – political, economic or social. By 'right' we mean the support of a more or less hierarchical social order and an opposition to change towards equality".[27]

"Right": who tries to stabilize and preserve the respective centers of power (e.g. monarchy, economic elites) and the structures on which this power is based (e.g. church, colonialism, slavery, corporate capitalism).

"Left": who advocates the recognition of the equality of all human beings and for a democratic containment of power.[28]

The French philosopher Geoffroy de Lagasnerie defines "left" as follows:[29]

"To define the left, I increasingly rely on a term from Sartre – authenticity. I believe that the point is to be authentic in one's relationship to the world, to free oneself from all the preconditions that define one's own situation. One must not bend oneself, one must not gloss over the re-

---

27 Lipset, S. M., Lazarsfeld, P. F., Barton, A. H., & Linz, J. (1954). The psychology of voting: An analysis of political behavior. Handbook of social psychology, 2, 1124-1175
28 Rainer Mausfeld, from the slides of the presentation at the DAI Heidelberg
29 https://www.republik.ch/2019/01/14/das-ist-nicht-neoliberalismus-das-ist-klassenkampf (translated from German)

Ultimately, these definitions can be reduced to two fundamentally different conceptions: "right": Humans are minors and must be controlled and educated by a ruling power. "left": Humans are of age and must be as free as possible.

Liberalism:

> *"Liberalism (Latin liber "free"; liberalis "concerning freedom, liberal") is a fundamental position of political philosophy and a historical and contemporary movement that strives for a liberal political, economic and social order. Liberalism emerged from the English revolutions of the 17th century."*[30]

> *"For the first time in many countries, nation states and democratic systems emerged from liberal citizen movements."*[31]

Historical liberalism essentially meant the liberation of the bourgeoisie from the rule of the church and aristocracy. In particular, liberalism plays an extremely important role in the emergence of modern capitalism and the history of the United States. Lierre Keith, co-author of the book *Deep Green Resistance*, explains the history of liberalism in dept in the chapter *Liberals and Radicals*:[32]

> *"(…) classical liberalism was the founding ideology of the US, and the values of classical liberalism — for better and for worse — have dispersed around the globe. The ideology of classical liberalism developed against the hegemony of theocracy. The king and church had all the economic, political, and ideological power. In bringing that power down, classic liberalism helped usher in*

---

30 Ralf Dahrendorf: Liberalism. In John Eatwell/Murray Milgate/Peter Newman (Hrsg.): The Invisible Hand. The New PalgraveMacmillan, London 1989, S. 183.
31 Christoph Nonn: Bismarck: Ein Preuße und sein Jahrhundert. C.H.Beck, München 2015, S. 123 ff. (Kap.: Die englische Alternative)
32 https://deepgreenresistance.net/en/resistance/liberals-radicals/liberals-radicals/

the radical analysis and political movements that followed. But the ideology has limits, both historically and in its contemporary legacy.

"The original founding fathers of the United States were not after a human rights utopia. They were merchant capitalists tired of the restrictions of the old order. The old world had a very clear hierarchy. This basic pattern is replicated in all the places that civilizations have arisen. There's God (sometimes singular, sometimes plural) at the top, who directly chooses both the king and the religious leaders. These can be one and the same or those functions can be split. Underneath them are the nobles, the priests, and the military. (...) Beneath them are the merchants, traders, and skilled craftsmen. The base of the pyramid contains the bulk of the population: people in slavery, serfdom, or various forms of indenture. And all of this is considered God's will, which makes resistance that much more difficult psychologically. Standing up to an abuser — whether an individual or a vast system of power — is never easy. Standing up to capital "G" God requires an entirely different level of courage, which may explain why this arrangement appears universally across civilizations and why it is so intransigent.

"In the West, one of the first blows against the Divine Right of Kings was in 1215, when some of the landed aristocracy forced King John to sign Magna Carta. It required the king to renounce

some privileges and to respect legal procedures. (...) Magna Carta plunged England into a civil war, the First Baron's War. (...)

"The American Revolution can be seen as another Baron's revolt. This time it was the merchant-barons, the rising capitalist class, waging a rebellion against the king and the landed gentry of England. They wanted to take the king and the aristocrats out of the equation, so that the flow of power went God→property owners. When they said 'All men are created equal,' they meant very specifically white men who owned property. That property included black people, white women, and more generally, the huge pool of laborers who were needed to turn this continent from a living landbase into private wealth. (...) Under the rising Protestant ethic, amassing wealth was a sign of God's favor and God's grace. God was still operable, he'd just switched allegiance from the old inherited powers to the rising mercantile class.

"Classical liberalism values the sovereignty of the individual, and asserts that economic freedom and property rights are essential to that sovereignty. John Locke, called the Father of Liberalism, made the argument that the individual instead of the community was the foundation of society. He believed that government existed by the consent of the governed, not by divine right. But the reason government is necessary is to defend private property, to keep people from steal-

ing from each other. This idea appealed to the
wealthy for an obvious reason: they wanted to
keep their wealth. From the perspective of the
poor, things look decidedly different. The rich
are able to accumulate wealth by taking the labor of the poor and by turning the commons into
privately owned commodities; therefore, defend-
ing the accumulation of wealth in a system that
has no other moral constraints is in effect de-
fending theft, not protecting against it. Classical
liberalism from Locke forward has a contradic-
tion at its center. It believes in human
sovereignty as a natural or inalienable right, but
only against the power of a monarchy or other
civic tyranny. By loosening the ethical constraints that had existed on the wealthy, classical liberalism turned the powerless over to the
economically powerful, simply swapping the
monarchs for the merchant-barons. Adam
Smith's The Wealth of Nations, published in
1776, provided the ethical justification for unbri-
dled capitalism."

In the meantime, capitalism and the mercantile class
have conquered the whole world. *Money rules the world,*
as we all know.

The liberal ideology and its underlying individualism has
proven itself as one of the most effective instruments of
power, because people who believe that they are free
will not resist.

> *"I freed hundreds of slaves. And I would have freed hundreds more if they but known they were slaves"*

said Harriet Tubman. Yet the first step toward *real* freedom comes with the radical analysis:[33]

> *"One of the cardinal differences between liberals — those who insist that Everything Will Be Okay — and the truly radical is in their conception of the basic unit of society. This split is a continental divide. Liberals believe that a society is made up of individuals. Individualism is so sacrosanct that, in this view, being identified as a member of a group or class is an insult. But for radicals, society is made up of classes (economic ones in Marx's original version) or any groups or castes. In the radical's understanding, being a member of a group is not an affront. Far from it; identifying with a group is the first step toward political consciousness and ultimately effective political action."*

The basic problems today are still essentially the same as in the famous story of Robin Hood, which takes place at the time of the above mentioned Magna Carta: The rich oppress the poor and steal from them. But by now, a huge pile of ideology has been added to justify this oppression and theft.

---

33   https://deepgreenresistance.net/en/preface/deep-green-resistance/

Neoliberalism:

During the 20th century, liberalism has emerged into neoliberalism, which has been described by Rainer Mausfeld as

> *"the most powerful and sophisticated indoctrination system a political ideology has ever seen".*[34]

> *"Neoliberalism, unlike traditional capitalism, is (...) from the beginning consciously twinned with a massive formation of ideology. It was clear to the founding fathers — who came from very different fields — of that what constitutes neoliberal ideology today, that this program is never feasible democratically.*

> *"So they knew — and Hayek explicitly says it — that they have to conquer the language, they have to conquer the brains. Neoliberalism depends on that more than any other ideology. More than any, including communism. One can say in all other things that there is something positive behind it, even though it has been betrayed and might be something completely different now.*

> *"Neoliberalism, 'take it from below and give it to the top,' as a gigantic redistribution programme, was from the beginning geared towards extreme formation of ideology. And it is so ingenious and so refined — it goes back to Lippman, Bernays and so on — that they have consciously devel-*

---

34   https://www.youtube.com/watch?v=mdchIFjToG8 (translated from German)

oped techniques, so that what today is called the neoliberal self is so highly fragmented and actually consists only of false identities. The identity is, ideally, their Facebook account, the smartphone they use, the car they drive, the type of Rolex they wear, the food they eat and so on. Identities have become market products that can be bought. This fragmentation has the advantage that an integral self, which could be a core of resistance, is actually no longer there in a totalitarian structure, because the grown social solidarity no longer exists.

"I am part of a community only through solidarity with others. But if I no longer identify myself with others as a community, but with market products, then solidarity will also be destroyed.

"...neoliberalism has from the beginning actually stressed the importance of [destroying] our psychological resistance to the decomposition of society, which was explicit when Thatcher said "there is no community". There is only a pile of atomized individuals and their task is to optimize their individual use as best they can. Everyone is a small "Me Inc." and if someone fails, he/she was just a poor "Me Inc." – that's what the market regulates – [...] and if someone succeeds, he/she has adapted well to the market. So neoliberalism is a kind of infamous combination and not just an economic program. Neoliberalism is totalitarian in the sense that — Thatcher

At the beginning of the 20th century, the famous catastrophe of the Titanic has already shown us in strong pictures and metaphors how this technocracy will end. In neoliberalism, the upper classes are still dancing, while the lower classes are already drowning. Those on top don't know (and don't want to know) how those below are doing.

The ideology rains down from top to bottom:

They don't want to see that the whole ship is already sinking.

With the words of Max Wilbert:

---

35 Rainer Mausfeld: https://www.youtube.com/watch?v=mdchIFjToG8 (translated from German)

It's time for a global uprising. The lower classes should organize and turn their gaze — and their weapons — to the top.

Our common goal must be to deprive the rich of their ability to steal from the poor and the powerful of their ability to destroy the planet.

Stand up.

36 https://dgrnewsservice.org/resistance/strategy/towards-a-revolutionary-ecology-an-interview-with-max-wilbert

THE WISDOM OF THE TOADS

I want to tell you a story. A story about permaculture, food chains, friendship, love and death. People are storytellers. We transport information through stories, or narratives, to use the more sophisticated term.

Actually I wanted to go with my good friend Cengiz to a political event, a meeting of the initiative *aufstehen* (stand up) about the resistance of the yellow vests in France. However, Cengiz decided to spend the evening with his newly hatched chicks, his cats and a good friend whom he looks after because she has addiction problems. He is one of the finest characters I have ever met. I taught him how to kill. We have already taken the lives of many proud roosters together.

At the same time, I have never met a person who cares more about his animal friends than he does.

Without him, I had no desire to go to the event. I wanted to spend such a wonderful spring evening in the garden. That was a good thing, because I think I learned much more there.

I heard voices all around me. It was the voices of the toads that migrated from the forest into my garden to perform their ecstatic mating rituals.

The three ponds I have built over the last few years were suddenly full of toads, talking loudly to each other. I consider it a great honor that they lay their eggs in my ponds.

Derrick Jensen says:

> *"So many indigenous people have said to me that the fundamental difference between western and indigenous ways of being is that even the most open-minded westerners generally view listening to the natural world as a metaphor, as opposed to the way the world really is."*

Listen. In medieval fairy tales, toads are a symbol of wisdom. In many tales there is the hero who suddenly understands the language of the animals after a magical initiation event. Medieval people still had a relationship to the natural world and an understanding of the wonders of life. What the toads tell me is that whether we call ourselves quite immodest Homo sapiens sapiens, the wisest of wise, wolves, bears, bison, toads or any of a thousand other names, we are all sitting on the same boat.

The world speaks. They all speak. The chicks who are calling for food. The toads with their mating cries. Trees communicate with each other and certainly with us. If we had not forgotten how to listen and if, as members of this culture, we had not largely given up our empathy, we could never allow this mass murder to happen.

It was not right to exterminate the wolves. The only way we can all permanently exist together is to recognize the needs and lives of others as as important as our own lives and needs. Moreover, life is sacred. All life.

This is, in my understanding, the core statement of permaculture, and the only way for us and all other species to survive.

We can fantasize all we want about colonizing Mars or other planets. All this is pure technocratic ideology. It has never worked. We are still all on the same boat.

The toads are much smaller than the ones I saw 10 years ago. Through the war of our culture against insects, we are depriving them of food. Insects are the animal basis of the food chain. To exterminate them is an abysmal stupidity and will cost us dearly.

Last year, I wanted to participate in the toad rescue operations that environmentalists carry out every spring. The toads have to cross roads on their way to their spawning grounds; the toad rescuers collect them in buckets and carry them safely across the road.

Last year, the toad rescue was canceled because there were too few toads.

They live in warlike conditions, but life wants to live. They still migrate, sing, mate and lay their eggs.

I had to think of the film *Life is a Miracle* by Serbian director Emir Kusturica, which takes place during the Bosnian War. The protagonist wants to commit suicide after his son was taken prisoner of war. But then the Serbian militia hands him a young Muslim woman as hostage, with whom he falls in love. They sleep together while bombs fall in the background.

Life wants to live.

Recently I killed two quails. It was hard. I cut their heads off with sharp poultry scissors. The eyes and beak opened a few more times in shock. The little body twitched in my left hand in agony. I cried. Then I plucked them, gutted them and ate them. It was the best meal I've had in months.

If you are a self-sufficient chicken farmer, you usually have to perform the ritual of slaughter only once a year. In autumn, you kill the surplus roosters and the hens that no longer lay.

Since all my wonderful chickens, turkeys and also my young peacock were massacred this winter by a hungry marten, I have given up breeding chickens for the time being and now try quails.

Quails are smaller, but they are much more efficient feed converters and have a better ratio of body size to egg size.

All processes are much faster in quails than in chickens, which means for me that I will have more meat more often, which in turn means that I will have to kill much more often.

I breed them in my incubator, I raise them, I feed them. Like all children, they are always hungry. They always want to eat and grow so fast that I can almost watch them getting bigger. With big, intelligent eyes they look at me and shout "Feed us, feed us", as little chicks all over the world call out to their parents. They scream for life. I love these little, sweet, intelligent birds and I love raising them. Most of them I will slaughter and eat one day.

I often feel like a cannibal eating his own children. But so is the harsh reality, adult knowledge, true wisdom: As long as we live on this earth, we consume the lives of others. Even the great Homo sapiens sapiens is biologically nothing but an animal. And as such, we are part of the archaic food chain that we in the west destroy so diligently.

The whole history of the world is the history of eating and being eaten. One can explain the whole world in food chains, and understanding food chains means understanding the world. The real world, not the artificial structure of civilization that we have created from ideologies, slavery and exploitation. Civilized people tend to think they can cross any natural boundaries, including food chains. A fatal error.

I consider vegetarianism and especially the extreme form, veganism, to be fundamentally wrong. I myself grew up mostly as a vegetarian, fortunately only from an age of about 8 years. I understand the moral arguments very well, but my body always said something different. I always had a ravenous appetite for meat, and stuffed it into myself wherever opportunity presented itself. I think I might have grown bigger and stronger if I had consumed more meat as a child.

Vegetarianism and veganism are modern phenomena with a religious character. The way our culture is treating our fellow creatures is a sin, without any doubt. But the vegan is pulling out of the affair, washes his or her hands in innocence and often tries to convert others with religious zeal and a moral club.

Never before has a human society existed that could do without animal products. The Inuit, who consume almost exclusively raw meat and fish (*Eskimo* means *raw meat eater*) have the best results in blood panels ever measured in humans.

A friend of mine and her daughter, both of whom have been vegetarians (not even vegans) for several years, have very poor blood panel results. The doctor explained two options: either eat meat, or take a handful of vitamin supplements every morning. The 21 year old daughter chose the latter for moral reasons. She is an attractive young woman, but her pale skin and glassy eyes speak of malnutrition.

One last argument: Does any of you know a second generation vegetarian or vegan?

I met one once. A three year old girl, whose mother was a very dogmatic vegan. Even her shoes featured the inscription "VEGAN" in capital letters. Her little daughter was severely physically and mentally handicapped, could hardly speak, had glassy, squinting eyes and such weak bones that her legs had grown crooked and she could not walk.

On my stove, the bones of the slaughtered quails simmer slowly for a long time to later feed my own as nutritious broth.

I think that this woman will never free herself from the vegan ideology, because if she had to admit what she did to her daughter she would have to spend the rest of her life in the hell of immeasurable guilt.

We all have to eat.

I can't imagine a more intimate relationship than eating someone else. Your flesh becomes mine. We unite. This must be seen as a sacred act.

The least I have to do is to give my quails the best possible living conditions. And I don't think it would be an exaggeration to worship them with rituals as holy animals. Haven't indigenous people always done this, with salmon, bison, and many other animals that were their food source before the Europeans exterminated them (the salmon, the bison, and the native humans...)?

When I take someone else's life to eat or otherwise utilize him or her, I am responsible for the wellbeing of that species. Both for moral reasons and for pure self-interest. I want to continue eating in the future.

Seriously, I think that a hunter-gatherer culture is the most respectful way of dealing with our fellow creatures. Stable natural communities from which healthy, strong, wild animals can be hunted when needed, to whom appropriate respect is shown in cult and ritual.

I would like to hunt, and in a healthy culture I would certainly be a hunter. But the completely degraded ecosystems no longer allow this. Animal husbandry therefore is a necessary compromise.

From a permaculture perspective, the final solution of a reasonable culture would be a large-scale and worldwide ecological restoration, solely for reasons of morality and justice. The restoration of habitats and the transition to a respectful, strictly taboo- and ritual-regulated extraction by hunting as source for meat.

If, for example, the American prairies with their 100 million murdered bison were restored, humans could have a considerable amount of high-quality bison meat every year, without the enormous ethical problems and environmental hazards of factory farming.

Currently, the United States spend about 69 million dollars *per hour* to finance its gigantic military apparatus. In Germany, this sum amounts to a paltry 5,023 thousand dollars per hour and rising.[37] If we would spend these gigantic sums not for imperialism, war, murder and destruction, but for ecological restoration and thus for the future of our children, projects like the vital cleaning and regeneration of the oceans and the regeneration of healthy, game rich forests, meadows and prairies would appear quite feasible.

Unfortunately, our culture seems to strive for the apocalypse as the final solution.

Preventing it from destroying the food chains and ultimately all life on the planet must be our common and most sacred duty. For moral reasons, for reasons of justice and for pure self-interest. Because we all have to eat. Now an in the future.

For further reading: The best books I know about food are Richard Mannings "Against the Grain", Lierre Keiths "The Vegetarian Myth" and Michael Pollans "The Omnivore's Dilemma".

---

37 https://de.statista.com/statistik/daten/studie/157935/umfrage/laender-mit-den-hoechsten-militaerausgaben/

[Boris Forkel is a radical environmentalist, social rights activist and subsistence farmer. The books he publishes with his press BabylonApocalypse inspire and encourage dissidents to break through an increasingly narrow public discourse and spread the seeds of decisive resistance and radical social change.]

Learn more about Deep Green Resistance:

www.DeepGreenResistance.org

Find a growing number of radical books:

www.BabylonApocalypse.org

Do something! Find what you love and defend your beloved. Everything is under assault.

Good luck!

Space for your notes

www.ingramcontent.com/pod-product-compliance
Lightning Source LLC
Chambersburg PA
CBHW051826250726

48659CB00005B/1698